Guide to Leading Intrapreneurs

Contents

Leading a large company that fosters intrapreneurship 3

How Large Companies Innovate 6

The Concept of Intrapreneurship 9

Examples of Intrapreneurship in some Large Corporations 12

Strategic Portfolio Management 17

Innovation Portfolio Management 20

Budgeting for Innovation 24

Innovation Metrics 27

Funding Criteria for Intrapreneurial Projects 30

Important Traits of an Intrapreneur 32

Traits of a Project Team Leader 35

Role of the Executive Sponsor 38

Motivating and Leading Intrapreneurs 40

About the Author 45

Leading a large company that fosters intrapreneurship

Usually CEOs of large companies need a partner for innovation inside their companies, someone who will encourage radical ideas and find new areas for growth. It's an innovation leader who can help the company reinvent itself while it is still successful. The goal is to increase shareholder value and long-term revenues.

This Innovation leader is responsible for developing new business models and value propositions for the company's future growth. They are responsible for creating the environment for your employees to experiment, fail, and learn. They are to develop the necessary culture, processes, incentives, and metrics. They are to develop indicators that measure whether the company is making progress in building new businesses by reducing uncertainty and risk. They are to work with the CEO and CFO to ensure resources and assets are available to validate innovative ideas. They are to deliver validated business models that demonstrate opportunities to scale. This Innovation leader is in charge of managing intrapreneurs, and is often known as an Executive Sponsor.

Sometimes the CEO acts as the facilitator of intrapreneurship instead of having an Innovation leader as a go-between. The CEO provides intrapreneurs the support, guidance, resources and an environment to innovate, by directly supervising them. The CEO places intrapreneurs where their strengths can have the most impact within the innovation framework of the company. Very few large companies have this model.

Four key factors that can help in creating an intrapreneurial climate in your company:

1. Organizational flexibility
2. Motivation and encouragement ethics
3. Resource management and distribution
4. Employee development opportunities

Four key factors that can beget skills for intrapreneurship in your company:

1. Harness the natural strength of innovators
2. Add fresh intrapreneurial perspectives through new recruits
3. Create different webs of innovators
4. Allocate specific tasks to intrapreneurs based on their skills

Encourage innovation in your company, allocate a good portion of your revenues towards intrapreneurial projects, constantly look for new projects that fit your strategy or are an extension of your strategy, reward intrapreneurs financially and emotionally, create a culture of intrapreneurship inside your company, let your employees spend a portion of their time working on pet projects, pardon failures, encourage speedy delivery, hire people with entrepreneurial experiences, encourage leaders who can take risks and make decisions, set up a formal process for commercializing select new ideas, and focus on the next decade's worth of revenue growth.

Corporate organizational structures such as bureaucracy, hierarchy, rules etc. usually do not support intrapreneurial culture and behavior.

How Large Companies Innovate

Large companies can innovate through corporate ventures, intellectual property licensing, alliances, acquisitions, internal skunkworks projects, and spinouts. How a company decides to commercialize an invention determines the success of the project. The choices made at various stages during the lifecycle of the project have to fit with the core business strategy. Innovation is not limited to technological innovation.

The Executive Sponsor is responsible for overseeing the following activities in a large corporation:

- Assemble a workforce that is diverse in education, experiences and talents
- Create a culture of innovation, encouraging risk-taking and failing fast
- Recognize and reward inventions made by employees
- Spot new opportunities from prospect needs/problems
- Select a project team leader for the innovation project
- Design new customer solutions, products, business models
- Optimize innovation portfolios and prioritize opportunities
- Prototype and pilot new innovation projects

- Encourage testing and learning
- Minimize uncertainty and risks
- Scale promising new projects

Corporate leaders put in a series of systems and a culture where the expectation is that if there's an idea that someone's passionate about, it is easy, fast and cheap for them to run an experiment.

You need great leaders to promote a culture of experimentation. Steve Jobs was one of those amazing people who could do that. He was willing to cannibalize his iPod revenues, which were $5 billion a year, by putting the entire mp3 player in every phone. Larry Page is doing that at Google. He's willing to invest in Google X, where they'll work on bold new projects. And they'll put $500 million toward that, like toward the self-driving car.

Some Intrapreneurial Successes:
- Apple created the Mac, iPod, iTunes, iPhone, iCloud
- Google created Gmail, Google News, AdSense, driverless cars, Google Glass, etc.
- Vanguard created an automated, web-based, robo-advising Personal Advisor Services
- GE created GE Digital, a unit that assimilates the company's digital

capabilities so that GE and its customers can connect to the industrial Internet of Things

According to Deloitte Consulting, every company should not only exploit and optimize their current products, but also harness innovation for lasting growth and profitability. They presented the following insights on Intrapreneurship:

- Intrapreneurship describes a people-centric, bottom-up approach to develop radical innovations in-house
- Intrapreneurship pays off many times in terms of company growth, talent and culture
- It is not about creating intrapreneurs, but finding and recognizing them
- Intrapreneurs know the rules and break them effectively
- Intrapreneurship requires a different management approach

The Concept of Intrapreneurship

Pinchot coined the term "intrapreneurship" in 1978. In his paper, named *intra-corporate entrepreneurship*, thus the name intrapreneurship, he points out that firms, in order to grow and prosper in a rapidly changing society and economy need entrepreneurial thinking within the company.

According to Knight these characteristics are innovativeness and proactiveness.
Innovativeness is defined as —the pursuit of creative or novel solutions to challenges confronting the firm, including the development or enhancement of products and services, as well as new techniques and technologies for performing corporate functions. Proactiveness is regarded as the aggressive posturing towards competitors, emphasizing execution and follow through with the attempt to achieve the company's goals.

One relatively recent research about intrapreneurship refers not only to the creation of new business ventures, but also to other innovative activities and orientations such as development of new products, services, technologies, strategies and competitive positions.

According to Thornberry, the different types of Corporate Entrepreneurship are: Corporate

Venturing, Intrapreneuring, Organizational Transformation and Industry Rule Breaking. Corporate venturing comprises of starting a business within a business, in most cases based on a company's core competency but also on innovation through new product development. Intrapreneuring is meant to instill the behavior and mindset of independent entrepreneurs in the firm's employees and thus create an innovative environment within the firm.

Organizational Transformation is the transforming and remodeling of the corporation; limited to the transformation processes that involve innovation, which might help the firm seize new opportunities.

Lastly, industry rule-bending deals with changing the rules of competitive engagement as yet another way of transformation.

Similar to other researchers, Heinonen & Korvela's core definition of intrapreneurship is again that of entrepreneurial measures of action within an established company. The authors stress two core competencies of the phenomenon of intrapreneurship.

The first is a company's commitment to innovation. This competency is however again divided into 3 subparts: product innovation, proactiveness and risk taking. Product innovation is described to be a company's ability to create new or modify products. Proactiveness refers to a company's ability to compete in the market by taking a pioneering role. Lastly, risk taking describes a company's attitude towards engaging in uncertain business venture or the like.

The second dimension of intrapreneurship Heinonen & Korvela discuss is strategic renewal, which is also divided into several subparts: mission reformation, reorganization and system-wide changes. Mission reformation refers to the renewal achieved through the redefinition of a firm's mission through the creative redeployment of resources. Reorganization refers to the dimension of renewal achieved by developing and/or adopting new corporate structures which encourage innovation. System-wide changes, that mostly target a company's core values, are supposed to bring about an enhancement in problem solving and creative learning, and thus cover the last part of the dimension of renewal.

Examples of Intrapreneurship in some Large Corporations

Here are seven examples of companies that successfully promoted intrapreneurship:

1. Lockheed Martin
Idea: It wouldn't be a post about intrapreneurship without the famous "Skunk Works" project. Skunk Works is another name for Advanced Development Programs or ADP. Lockheed Martin basically allowed Kelly Johnson, Skunk Works founder, to work as an autonomous organization with a small, focused team.
Benefit: Skunk Works created some of the most innovative aircraft models, including the SR71. Moral of the story: if you have an intrapreneur like Johnson in your organization, don't fight back. Instead, give them the support and resources they need to thrive. Lockheed Martin learned early that successful intrapreneurship happens when team members are allowed to define a clear path with their idea and they are given the power to modify and innovate as needed without a crazy approval process.

2. Texas Instruments
Idea: A TI researcher, Larry Hornbeck, had been experimenting with technology using tiny mirrors to redirect photons for almost a decade. In 1987, Hornbeck and his team developed Digital Micromirror Device. DMD was used for

printing airline tickets at first but soon after TI started an internal venture called Digital Imaging Venture Project to expand on the efforts.

Benefit: For a long time, video projectors weighed the equivalent to a small child and cost upwards of $15,000. Hornbeck realized this technology could greatly decrease the size and cost of the digital projector and it soon became an industry standard. He even received an Emmy award for Outstanding Achievement in Engineering Development, talk about some serious intrapreneurial bragging rights.

3. Google

Idea: Google allows time for personal projects. Some of Google's best projects come out of their 20 percent time policy. One of these is something you probably use multiple times a day, Gmail.

Benefit: Paul Buchheit, the creator of Gmail, started on the project in 2001 and worked up to its launch on April 1, 2004 (April Fools but not really.) Gmail became the first email with a successful search feature and the option to keep all of your email (hello 1GB of storage) instead of frantically deleting to stay under your limit. The initial launch was by invite only, quite the hot commodity. Now, it's considered a faux pas not to have an email address ending in @gmail.com.

4. 3M

Idea: Sometimes, intrapreneurship happens by accident. Dr. Spencer Silver, a scientist at 3M, was attempting to create an extremely strong adhesive to use in aerospace technology. Instead, he accidentally created a light adhesive that stuck to surfaces well but didn't leave a nasty residue.

Benefit: Instead of throwing away this idea because it didn't solve the problem at hand, he stuck with it until he found a use for it. After many years of persistence and spreading the word it finally clicked with someone else, Art Fry—another 3M scientist. He thought back to one of Silver's seminars and they began to develop a product together. Post-It notes were born and if you are the vast majority of desk workers you're probably looking at a pad of them right now.

5. Sun Microsystems

Idea: Patrick Naughton, a developer, almost left Sun in 1995 because he believed they were missing out on the fast-growing PC consumer market. He was convinced to stay and help Sun set up a group dedicated to the consumer market. This is where group member, James Gosling, created an elegant object-oriented programming language called Oak, which was later renamed Java.

Benefit: This was initially created to help set up Time Warner cable boxes. When that deal fell through, Bill Joy, co-founder of Sun, recognized the value of Java and that it could be implemented across all different platforms. As you know, Sun has since merged into Oracle and Java now runs the world with 930 million Java Runtime Environment downloads each year and 3 billion mobile phones run on Java.

6. Facebook
Idea: Originally called the "awesome button," the Facebook Like button was first prototyped in one of
Facebook's infamous hack-a-thons.
Benefit: Facebook has never released statistics based on the like rate and certain time frames. But to all of us in the computer using world it is pretty evident how the invention of the like button affects us on a daily basis. Companies like Facebook, who are constantly innovating and changing, are some of the most successful out there.

7. Sony
Idea: Ken Kutaragi, a relatively junior Sony Employee, spent hours tinkering with his daughter's Nintendo to make it more powerful and user friendly. What came from his work is one of the most recognizable brands in the world today, The Sony Playstation.
Benefit: Many Sony bosses were outraged at his work, thinking that gaming is a complete waste of time. Luckily someone in a senior position saw the value in the product and thankfully so, because now Sony is one of the world leaders in the prosperous gaming industry. This shows that company leaders should always be open to

innovation—no matter how farfetched and pointless it may seem.

Strategic Portfolio Management

The Boston Consulting Group Matrix depicts four quadrants that distinguish high and low markets and a product's position in those markets. The products are grouped as "stars," "cash cows," "dogs," and "question marks." Stars, which are dominant products in a growing market, and cash cows, which are legacy products that control a steady or diminishing market, make up the bulk of profitability for a company. Dogs are low-yielding products in a declining market that drain resources and are contenders for elimination. Product decisions are most difficult around question marks, which are products that have some level of potential for innovation in a market that is growing.

General Electric and McKinsey Consulting expanded and adapted the BCG Matrix to suit its diverse product families and numerous acquisitions. It uses "Industry Attractiveness" and "Business Unit Strength" to anchor its X-Y Matrix. The Low-Medium-High ratings give a broader view of products in order to identify those to develop, markets to expand into, products to re-tool, and products to eliminate.

Scoring and mapping methods, as well as matrix and bubble charts, provide data and visualizations to help make the decisions for effective product portfolio management. You can also add weight to other elements such as experience, common sense, or educated guesses.

Innovation portfolios are not for product innovation alone. They also include process, service, and business model innovation. Many companies also track external innovations in which they have invested, or have options to pick up. Issues such as riskiness, likely benefits, and relevance to different business units, functions or markets are considered.

On average, high-performing firms direct 70% of their innovation resources to enhancements of core offerings, 20% to adjacent opportunities, and 10% to transformational initiatives. But individual firms may deviate from that ratio for sound strategic reasons. A mid-stage technology firm may want to devote 45% to core, 40% to adjacent and 15% to transformational initiatives.

These are the questions you need to answer while managing a portfolio of businesses in a large company: What is the fundamental potential of each business in terms of the markets served, growth, margin, and competitive advantage? What is the value to the company of each business today and what will it be in the future? What is the contribution to share price, market capitalization, and the future valuation multiple? Does the portfolio have an appropriate mix of businesses that offer short-term growth and long-term growth? Are there enough cash-generating businesses to fund growth businesses? Is the portfolio sensibly diversified in terms of business risk? Do the businesses fit the company's investment thesis and style of competition? Are there synergies across them? Can the businesses take advantage of the corporate center's assets or capabilities to create additional value? Is the value of the portfolio, taken as a whole, greater than the sum of the parts? Is the portfolio attractive to desired investors?

Innovation Portfolio Management

Innovation portfolio management can act as the pivotal tool to translate strategic objectives and priorities into project-based innovation activities. By allocating capital across a range of investments, you can obtain the best return while controlling risk. The key, as articulated in portfolio theory, is that the risks taken must be non-correlated.

The following criteria *could* belong on your list of criteria for innovation portfolio management:

- Fit with strategic factors
- Uniqueness
- Probability of technical success
- Probability of commercial success
- R&D cost to completion or to next milestone
- Time to completion or to next milestone
- Intellectual property protection
- Barriers to entry
- Durability of competitive advantage
- Innovation platform
- Timing in terms of competition and market demand
- Right balance of risk
- Team working on the project
- Product-market fit
- Technology trends
- Diversity of portfolio initiatives

- Resource availability

According to Ernst and Young, the following five groups include the most popular tools for innovation portfolio management:

1. Plot diagrams: this group of tools comprises bubble diagrams and priority risk diagrams. Many bubble diagrams can be traced back to the traditional Boston Consulting Group matrix, and they often involve two axes with dimensions referring to risk and reward. The size of bubbles typically indicates the number of projects in a given group. Priority-risk diagrams extend bubble diagrams with risk mitigation logic to estimate the portfolio risk and to consider the effects of adding new projects to the current innovation portfolio.

2. Decision systems: this set of tools includes decision trees and artificial neural network systems. Decision tree analyses often use financial value and risk data to generate future scenarios. In particular, decision tree models allow for considering multiple possible outcomes and for taking into account several sequential decisions. Artificial neural network systems constitute decision support systems that predict financial and technical success for new product projects to arrive at clear portfolio decisions concerning the initiation or termination of specific projects.

3. Scoring approaches: this collection of tools comprises scoring models and analytical hierarchy processes. Scoring models refer to ranking projects on various dimensions, e.g., risk, competencies, strategic fit and competition, which are weighted and aggregated to arrive at an overall score for each new product project. Scoring models enable managers to rely on a detailed list of criteria in a systematic way. Analytical hierarchy processes combine a scoring approach with constrained optimization logic to support complex decision-making.

4. Program illustrations: this group of tools includes strategic road maps and product innovation charters. Road maps refer to graphical illustrations of information to support long-term technology and market planning. Road mapping may further enhance communication and organizational learning because it helps to integrate the perspectives of multiple organizational departments, such as R&D and marketing. In addition, product innovation charters indicate target business areas as well as specific objectives and development programs to ensure active innovation strategies.

5. Expenditure analyses: this set of tools involves strategic buckets and sensitivity analyses. Strategic buckets describe top-down strategies for innovation expenditures to ensure simultaneous and balanced investments in different project types, e.g., radical and incremental ideas, in line with corporate

strategy. Sensitivity analyses help to compare the maximum and minimum values of new product projects relative to a base value. Thus, these analyses help managers to deepen their understanding of project and portfolio outcomes under different internal and external conditions.

Valuation of the innovation portfolio should increase year over year. Some of the financial valuation approaches for later stage projects include NPV, asset valuation, and/or option value of work. Incremental innovation metrics might include tracking the percent of incremental revenue within existing product lines.

Budgeting for Innovation

The right amount of annual R&D reallocation for an individual company depends on its industry, strategy, and competitive situation. A steady, consistent level of R&D reallocation year after year is highly consistent with successful innovation at scale. In a fast-changing competitive environment, companies that succumb to resource inertia will struggle to meet their strategic goals.

Budgeting for innovation also depends to a large extent on where a company is in its lifecycle. If you are an innovative large company, you would spend 2% to 35% of your revenues on R&D, depending on your lifecycle and corporate strategy.

When executives were asked what they would want to pour money in, they replied:
- 75% on day-to-day operations
- 5% on incremental improvements
- 10% on sustaining innovations
- 10% on big, disruptive innovations

Innovation Budget Planning Considerations:

- Understand Your Market and the trends in markets, technologies and adjacent technologies
- Align Your R&D Strategy with your long-term corporate strategy

- Know Your R&D Capabilities to avoid inefficiencies or to promote use of outside resources
- Consider the market risk, technical risk and business model risk for each project
- Remember that 80% of your profits will come from 20% of your products
- Remember that the project may take a lot more money and time before it is a commercial success
- Assess what spending would be required for acquisitions and partnerships
- Plan for unstoppable technological and macroeconomic forces that may affect your company

It's too easy for revenue producing parts of the business to poach resources from innovation projects and teams that are not generating revenues. They need to be protected and made autonomous, with their own dedicated budgets, resources, and leadership, until they are.

Here is how you can prioritize and smooth the R&D process:

- Do less. Initiate fewer projects. Track fewer measures. Get better at ending "zombie" projects, those efforts that have failed but no one wants to declare dead.
- Allow the important to triumph over the urgent. Prioritize resources carefully.

> Create clear policies about who can launch new projects and rigorously hold sponsors accountable for outcomes.
- Take time before you reach for that fireman's helmet. More time spent early on to find the root cause of a problem can save money in symptom management later.

One approach to budgeting is to examine each new product or service at each stage of development to review if the project should be killed or not.

Another approach to budgeting is the Innovation Accounting approach, where you have three types of Innovation key performance indicators: Reporting KPIs, designed to track work as it moves from the idea stage to scale; Governance KPIs, so that companies can determine whether or not to continue to invest in a new venture; and Global KPIs, to examine the overall performance of an innovative idea in relation to the overall company.

Innovation Metrics

Metrics can drive behavior, as well as evaluate the results of specific initiatives. Some companies like 3M have tried to mandate that 35% of the corporations' revenues should come from products introduced within the past four years. In 2000, 10% of Procter and Gamble's R&D was outsourced, and today, 50% of all ideas and technology come from the outside.

Across the Fortune 1000, the most prevalent innovation metrics include:

- Annual R&D budget as a percentage of annual sales
- Number of patents filed in the past year
- Total R&D headcount or budget as a percentage of sales
- Number of active projects
- Number of ideas submitted by employees
- Percentage of sales from products introduced in the past X year(s)

In an environment in which disruptive innovation and cannibalization must be wholeheartedly embraced as a core strategy, new structures and related metrics are needed for driving behaviors. Too many metrics leads to excessive activities that provide little value and often drive conflicting behaviors.

Key Innovation Metrics

- % of capital invested in innovation activities such as submitting and reviewing ideas for new products and services
- % of capital invested in developing ideas through an innovation pipeline
- Percentage of "outside" vs. "inside" inputs to the innovation process (open innovation)
- Number of new products, services, and businesses launched in new markets in the past year
- Actual vs. targeted breakeven time
- % of revenue/profit from products or services introduced in the past X years
- Royalty and licensing income from patents/intellectual property
- % of employees who have received training and tools for innovation, e.g., instruction in estimating market potential of an idea
- Existence of formal structures & processes that support innovation
- Number of new competencies that spawn innovation
- Number of innovations that significantly advance existing businesses
- Number of new opportunities in new markets
- % of executives' time spent on strategic innovation versus day-to-day operations

- % of managers with training in the concepts and tools of Innovation
- Net Present Value of the Innovation project
- Internal Rate of Return of the Innovation project
- Economic Value Added of the Innovation project
- Discounted Cash Flow for the Innovation project
- Return on Investment for the Innovation project
- Risk of the Innovation project compared to the overall risk of the Innovation Portfolio

It is critical to engage key stakeholders in defining your metrics that will guide the corporation into the future.

Funding Criteria for Intrapreneurial Projects

In the face of drivers such as hyper-competition, technology disruption and new customer power, companies are increasingly looking to achieve growth from new non-core areas, requiring more focus on innovation, especially breakthrough innovation, in order to prosper. Innovative large companies invest in innovation across many functions, such as strategy, product development, management, marketing, sales, administration and finance.

If the intrapreneurial project has to do with new product development or adding a new service offering, these are the questions the Executive Sponsor would ask:

- What are the basic details of your innovation?
- What product/service do you plan to offer?
- Who would be your customers? How would they gain value from your offering?
- Who would be your competitors? How is the industry currently divided?
- What would give your product/service its competitive edge?

- How will you market and sell your product/service?
- What would be your most important operational features?
- Where are you in the technology development process?
- What would be the timeline for piloting/testing?
- Who would be the key members of your project team and what are their qualifications? Have you selected a project team leader?
- What are your long-term goals? What are some of the milestones you plan to meet?
- What would be the expected gross sales and net profits from this product/service?
- What are the project risks, and assumptions that you have made?
- Does this product/service fit in with the corporate strategy and innovation goals?
- How much money are you seeking from the executive sponsor, and how and when will the money be used?

Important Traits of an Intrapreneur

An Intrapreneur is a person within a large corporation who takes direct responsibility for turning an idea into a profitable finished product through assertive risk-taking and innovation. Intrapreneurs are gifted problem-solvers, adaptive opportunists, resourceful connectors, and humble.

Today, instead of waiting until the company is in a bind, most companies try to create an environment where employees are free to explore ideas. If the idea looks profitable, the person behind it is given
an opportunity to become an intrapreneur.

Intrapreneurs have an entrepreneurial spirit. They are dynamic in thought and action; they activate ideas and people, and are comfortable working in teams. They are committed to innovation, which means they feel that have to improve on something, or do something radically different. They are constantly improving on ideas. They are not afraid to change course. A good reward motivates them to take calculated risks. They do not think of competition as an obstacle. They are confident and can handle rejection, or failure. They behave authentically and with integrity. They respect and value money but are not lured by it in the way entrepreneurs are.

In addition to the above mentioned qualities, they are passionate, courageous, determined, resourceful, adaptable, results-driven, and diplomatic.

Advantages of Intrapreneuring over Entrepreneuring:

- Capital Sources
- Access to customers
- Infrastructure
- Management pools
- Leverage on an existing business
- Corporate reputation or brand
- Lower risk

Disadvantages of Intrapreneuring over Entrepreneuring:

- Reliance on sponsorship
- Corporate Profit and Loss focus
- Corporate meddling, bureaucracy, hierarchy, rules
- Lesser authority
- Lower monetary reward

Large corporations need to recognize and develop intrapreneurs, and, make sure they won't leave.

Traits of a Project Team Leader

Sometimes, the project champion/sponsor appoints a project team leader who is not the same person as the one who invented the idea. The Project team leader needs a good mix of technical, business and social skills, and is very necessary for the intrapreneurship project to succeed in the large company.

Leadership is most needed when the there is a high amount of change, uncertainty and volatility. Management involves dealing with complexity, and includes elements such as setting goals and budgets, establishing detailed steps, allocating resources, solving problems, and monitoring the results. Leadership involves dealing with change and includes such elements as setting and communicating direction, developing vision, and aligning team members, stakeholders, and others. The project manager is the most critical element for projects to be delivered successfully.

Project Manager Skills and Competencies in the right order are as follows:

1. People skills
2. Leadership
3. Listening
4. Integrity, ethical behavior, consistent

5. Strong at building trust
6. Verbal communication
7. Strong at building teams
8. Conflict resolution, conflict management
9. Critical thinking, problem solving
10. Understands, balances priorities

The three most important skills required for the project leader depend on the nature of the project:

- For a very large project, leadership, relevant prior experience and planning are important
- For a project with high uncertainty, risk management, expectation management, and leadership are important
- For a very novel project requiring a lot of innovation, leadership, people skills, and skills to do with vision, purpose and goals are important
- Depending on the project environment or the lifecycle of the project or the industry, a different set of skills may be important

The project team leader is responsible for communicating with the project sponsor, communicating with various stakeholders, setting clear objectives, project planning, motivating the project team, reporting, monitoring, controlling, managing uncertainty, aligning incentives, creating a culture of accountability, managing risk, making decisions, and achieving desired project outcomes.

Role of the Executive Sponsor

Intrapreneurs need to secure top executive sponsorship for their continued active support, political weight and funding. Executive sponsors are leaders who lead leaders (intrapreneurs).

As a leader of leaders, the executive sponsor does not tell the intrapreneur what to do. Instead they fire up vision and imagination. They allow intrapreneurs to own their decisions. They coach, influence, and converse with intrapreneurs.

The sponsor makes sure that the project's goals are aligned with overall company strategy. He/she garners support and overcomes resistance from other senior executives, and provides ongoing direction as the effort unfolds. In contrast with the project leader, who focuses mostly on day-to-day execution, the sponsor role is much more strategic, focusing on creating conditions for success instead of tactical implementation. In a large corporation, the executive may be a sponsor to dozens of projects and may be stretched for time. Thus, the role largely consists of skimming project review decks and occasionally signing off on a milestone. Before launching a new project, the sponsor and the project leader should meet to set, clarify, and align expectations.

The responsibilities for which the Sponsor is accountable to the Board are:

- Provides leadership on culture and values
- Owns the business case
- Keeps the project aligned with company's strategy and innovation goals
- Governs project risk
- Works with other sponsors
- Focuses on benefiting the company
- Recommends opportunities to optimize risk/reward
- Ensures continuity of sponsorship
- Provides insights and assurance

The Executive Sponsor takes the lead in establishing a budget and assigning the right resources for the project. They engage and create support with other senior managers. They take a lead role in building and maintaining a healthy coalition of leaders who support the intrapreneurial project.

Motivating and Leading Intrapreneurs

Several big companies today actively promote intrapreneurship, allowing their employees to spend 10%-20% of their time on innovative ideas that are unrelated to their normal work. This isn't about employees trying to do better at their existing jobs; this is them wanting to create something new that doesn't currently exist. Intrapreneurs can be a vital creative force to enter new markets, invent new products, strike new partnerships, and test new marketing approaches.

Design Thinking and human-centered design have proliferated, corporate accelerators and incubators are full of activity, and corporate innovators are proud to share their work.

Performing an innovation diagnostic provides insight into an organization's overall strengths and weaknesses, how its organizational structures and cultural aspects hinder or support innovation. Within the areas of strategy, process and organization, you can explore core competencies, conventions, implicit strategy and innovation systems.

Ideas are fragile and prone to pivot once they meet the market, whereas problems and teams are resilient and can stay intact through many pivots until the problem is solved. Share wins along the way, and lessons-learned on a regular basis, to help uncover keys to success as well as the recurring sticking points for project design.

It is not always easy to manage intrapreneurs. They can be disruptive, may invite conflict and mistrust, may bet the reputation of your company, may break corporate norms, and can be challenging to manage.

Here is how you can lead intrapreneurs in your company:

1. Make internal intrapreneurship part of the evaluation and reward process. Intrapreneurship must be seen as important not only as a value statement, but also by the metrics by which individuals are held accountable.

2. Assure there is money available to support scavenger activities. The combination of scavenging activity and formal project funding creates a high level of motivation and commitment in the company. Make sure that projects do not get unduly killed or suffocated.

3. Be clear about the criteria and standards by which intrapreneurial ideas will be judged. Set clear milestones. Establish norms for updates, and rules about what decisions the intrapreneur can take.

4. Give intrapreneurs the behavioral skills they need. They need to learn the political skills that will enable them to take ideas up the organization. They also need to learn about the company's priorities and the appropriate resources that are available to develop their ideas. Encourage them to challenge industry assumptions. Establish a culture of learning and experimentation in your company.

5. Focus on the right organizational design. Sterile, rigid bureaucracy is an intrapreneurial killer. While accountability and hierarchy are essential for organizational control, the corporate structure needs to be agile. Train high-potential intrapreneurs on innovation theory, and encourage them to study customers.

6. Recognize and reward intrapreneurs financially and emotionally. Give them the incentives to pursue their dreams.

7. Provide peer support. Intrapreneurs may feel isolated and disengaged from their colleagues and need to have avenues for support and

collaboration that make them feel engaged and able to drive value. Create a culture of velocity.

8. Collaborate across functions. Building and supporting intrapreneurs effectively requires a variety of functional groups within a large company to work together. Functions may include Innovation Programs, Training, C-suite, Business Unit leadership, etc. Make sure that there is sufficient and suitable communication between the intrapreneur and various stakeholders.

9. Channels and Processes. Some examples might include: time credit pools where people can be taken out of their role to work on new ideas for a period of time, idea funding pools, idea review and development channels, risk controls, etc.

10. Protect and enhance your company's reputation. Ensure that your intrapreneur has adequate understanding of your mainstream culture, products, and brand. Have an executive or senior manager sign-off on their marketing announcements before they go public. Consider branding any disruptive ideas under a separate entity name.

Senior leaders sponsoring innovation need to form a set of permissions at the level of an opportunity, distinct from the classic incremental improvement work that the company is familiar with. It requires a new set of behaviors in sponsors who advocate for possibilities like a VC would, rather than serving as a judge of what works.

About the Author

Ms. Hetal Shah is an expert in strategy, innovation, entrepreneurship and product management. She has over 10 years of professional work experience in the sales, marketing, operations, administrative and entrepreneurial fields. She has worked in the financial services, philanthropy, technology and management consulting sectors. She has worked for four technology startups in the past. She is knowledgeable about the software and telecommunications industries. She was born in 1972. She attained a bachelor's degree in Civil engineering from Bradley University in 1993. In 2001, she was a founder and CEO of a telecommunications-media startup in Boston. Now, she is a business coach and independent management consultant in Boston. She has lived in the Boston area for over 21 years. She is well-read about business, finance and entrepreneurship. She is looking for artificial intelligence, robotics, software and telecommunications companies as clients for her independent management consulting services. She can be reached at hetaliscoy@yahoo.com.

www.ingramcontent.com/pod-product-compliance
Lightning Source LLC
Chambersburg PA
CBHW031553210526
45464CB00003B/1289